How Co
How Se

THAT'S HOW THINGS BEGAN

teri
The Energy and Resources Institute

An imprint of The Energy and Resources Institute

First Reprint 2014 (Revised)
Second Reprint 2015
Third Reprint 2017

Published by
TERI Press
The Energy and Resources Institute
Darbari Seth Block, IHC Complex, Lodhi Road, New Delhi - 110 003, India
Tel. 2468 2100/4150 4900, Fax: 2468 2144/2468 2145
India +91 ■ Delhi (0)11
Email: teripress@teri.res.in ■ Website: http://bookstore.teri.res.in

ISBN 978-81-7993-547-7

Author: R P Subramanian
Publishing Head: Anupama Jauhry
Editorial and Production Teams: Ekta Sharma, Himanshi Sharma, Pallavi Sah, Yoofisaca Syngkon Nongpluh; Aman Sachdeva, Mahfooz Alam
Design and Illustration Teams: Priyabrata Roy Chowdhury, Santosh Gautam, Rajiv Sharma, and Vijay Kumar; Yatindra Kumar, Vijay Nipane, and Neeraj Riddlan
Image Researcher: Yukti Garg

Printed and bound in India

This book is printed on recycled paper.

CONTENTS

How did we learn to make fire?

We need fire every day. At home, we make fires for cooking food. In our factories and farms, we use fires to heat, melt, boil, or dry all kinds of things. We burn coal and oil in power stations to make electricity, which we use in our homes and workplaces. Imagine, then, a time when no one knew how to make fire!

Fuel is food for me.

Old flames

In early times, the only fire people saw was when lightning struck a tree and set it ablaze. But about one-and-a-half million years ago, people in Africa were making wood fires to cook meat. They rubbed certain kinds of dry sticks together till they caught fire. Later, people found they could produce sparks to start a fire by striking certain rocks, called flints, against pieces of iron. In South East Asian countries, people squeezed air inside a small bamboo tube (using a wooden plunger). This produced enough heat to start a fire!

Burnt flakes of flint have been found in northern Israel, suggesting that fire was discovered 790,000 years ago!

A matchstick slowly evolved into a wooden stick coated with a mixture containing phosphorus.

THAT'S HOW THINGS BEGAN

The first matches

In 1669, a German chemist named Hennig Brandt discovered white phosphorus, a new element that caught fire all by itself! But it was also very poisonous, making it too risky for people to use. One day in 1826, an English chemist named John Walker brushed a stick coated with some chemicals against some stones. To his surprise, the stick caught fire! In this way, Walker discovered the chemicals he needed to make the world's first matches. They were sold under the name "Lucifers" and became quite popular; but they crackled and smoked a lot.

Early man used fire for heat, light, tool-making, and cooking.

John Walker, an English chemist, made the world's first matches.

Eureka, we started a fire!

Safety matches

In 1845, Austrian chemist Anton von Schrötter discovered red phosphorus. It was much safer to use than white phosphorus. Ten years later, John Edvard Lundström of Sweden invented the first safety matches. In these matches, the chemicals that make fire are divided between the matchstick head and the striking surface. We use safety matches even today!

HOW LONG WILL THEY LAST?

In AD 577, a Chinese inventor coated little sticks of pinewood with sulphur to make "firesticks", which burst into flame at the slightest spark. These firesticks made it easier to make fires, but you still had to make a spark first!

How did we learn to tell time?

Like us, early humans found it very important to tell time; to know how much daylight remained for them to do all the things necessary for survival! At first, they guessed the time of day by seeing the Sun's position in the sky. But this was a very rough way of telling time.

Galileo Galilei, Italian astronomer and physicist

Sundials

Around 3000 BC, people in Babylon and Egypt invented the sundial. As the Sun moved across the sky, the shadow of an upright stick fell on different marks on a circular base to show the time. The sundial was fairly accurate but could tell time only during the day.

Is time running out?

Later, people invented the water clock. This was a bowl of water with a hole in its base. The level of water showed the time as water leaked out. The sandglass, or an hourglass, worked on the same principle. People also invented candle and oil-lamp clocks, in which the length of the candle or the level of oil showed the time. Such clocks could tell the time during night, too, but they were very inaccurate.

The level of sand in sandglasses indicated the passage of time.

Early civilizations, like the Babylonian and the Egyptian, depended on the Sun dial to tell time.

Mechanical clocks

In 1657, Dutch scientist Christian Huygens used the idea of Italian astronomer, Galileo Galilei, to make the first pendulum clock. In 1675, he made the first accurate watch using a "spiral balance" spring. This could be worn on a chain or around the wrist. The pendulum clocks and spring watches were quite accurate; they lost less than ten seconds per day.

Quartz watches and clocks

In 1927, Warren Marrison, an engineer with Bell Telephone Laboratories, United States, made the first quartz watch. A quartz crystal vibrates fifty thousand times a second; Marrison found a way to make these vibrations move the hands of his watch. Today, quartz watches and clocks are available all over the world. They are very accurate and lose only one second in ten years!

Swinging away!

The pendulum clock was designed by Galileo Galilei.

Swinging time

In 1583, Galileo watched a chandelier swing back and forth in the Cathedral of Pisa. He realized that each swing took the same time. Galileo had no watch; so he timed the swings with his own pulse-beat! This gave him the idea for a pendulum clock.

The modern quartz watches are very precise.

How did we learn to cross the oceans?

Oars made from wood

Over fifty thousand years ago, the Polynesians travelled from island to island across the Pacific Ocean, all the way to Australia. They used a type of boat called dugout, which was made by scooping out the inside of a log of wood.

A dugout made by scooping out the insides of a log

An early Egyptian boat, which used oars to help the boat move

Wind power

The Polynesians also learned to use wind power by inventing the sail. Their dugouts had a triangular sail attached to a vertical pole. The dugout was pushed by a paddle when there was no wind. Soon, Polynesians and other people learned to tie together two or more dugouts for a smoother ride. Such boats, called catamarans, are used till today in South and South East Asia.

Titanic tragedy

The Titanic was the most luxurious ocean liner of the 1900s. Sadly, on April 14, 1912, it struck an iceberg and sank, killing 1,595 people.

From oar boats to clippers

Invention of metal tools helped people cut and shape wood better; they were able to build better boats. But it was hard to push water with paddles! Around 1500 BC, the oar was invented. The oar made it much easier to push water when there was no wind.

The sail was improved over the centuries so that boats became bigger and were able to move much faster and for much longer distances than before. Trade grew by leaps and bounds between China, India, Arabia, Africa, and Europe. New lands were discovered; people and goods could travel faster by sailing ships across waters than over land. The greatest ever sailing ships were the clippers of the 1840s.

Clippers used by traders to ferry goods across oceans

A modern steamboat

From steamships to ocean liners

After James Watt improved the steam engine design in 1769, many people tried to design ships that could be driven by a steam engine rather than by wind. In 1807, American inventor Robert Fulton launched the first commercial steamboat service in the world. This ran between New York and Albany – a distance of 240 km, which took thirty-two hours! In 1884, Charles Parsons invented the steam turbine, which helped in getting much more power from steam. Today, turbine-powered ocean liners are like floating palaces: they have swimming pools, shops, restaurants, theatres, arcades, and lots more; some even carry over three thousand people!

A boat or yacht with two parallel hulls is a catamaran.

How did we find and use metals?

Melting metal under high temperatures

In early times, humans made simple tools and weapons from stone. Around 8000 BC, they discovered shiny rocks that did not chip or break when struck; instead, they bent at the edges! These rocks were actually lumps of pure metals like copper, gold, and iron. Unlike stone, these metal lumps (called nuggets) could be hammered into sheets to make tools, arrows, and jewellery. They could also be melted in charcoal fires and poured into moulds to make vessels. The copper, silver, and gold nuggets came from the Earth, but the iron nuggets were actually meteorites that had fallen from space!

Precious metal!

Copper, tin, and bronze

Around 5000 BC, people discovered that they could extract metals from certain kinds of rock, called ores, by roasting the ores with charcoal. This process is now called smelting. By smelting ores, people not only made copper but also discovered new metals like lead and tin. Soon, they made an alloy (metal mixture) called bronze by melting tin and copper together. Bronze was very strong, yet easy to shape into all kinds of objects.

Iron from ore

Although iron nuggets were rare, iron ore was easy to find. The problem was that ordinary charcoal fires weren't hot enough to smelt iron. Around 100 BC, the Chinese invented a furnace to smelt iron by blowing air into the mixture of ore and charcoal from below the fire. This "blast furnace" model was used for nearly eighteen hundred years.

Strength of steel.

Old is gold

Though gold is one of the rarest metals, it was the first to be discovered.

But charcoal, which is made from wood, kept getting costlier as forests were felled for farms and timber. People tried using coal instead of charcoal for smelting iron, but the sulphur in the coal weakened the iron. Finally, in 1709, Abraham Darby found a way to smelt iron using coke (which is made from coal).

Steel

In 1856, Henry Bessemer invented a furnace, called the Bessemer converter, to turn iron into an even tougher alloy called steel. Today, steel is used to make bridges, buildings, railways, cars, carriages, ships, machinery, and countless other things.

Copper ore

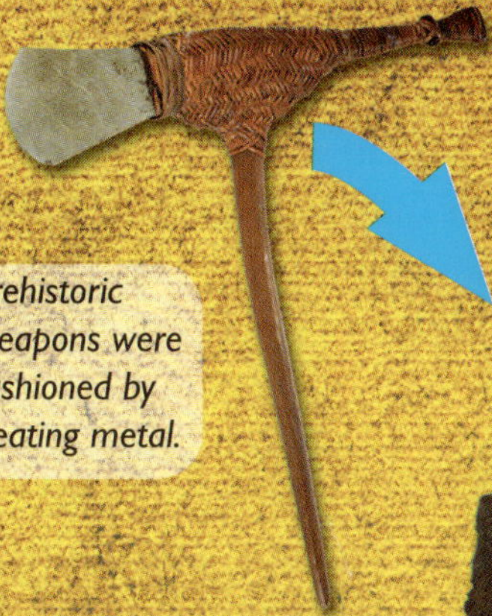

Prehistoric weapons were fashioned by beating metal.

The metal iron is extracted from iron ore.

The Bessemer converter was invented by Henry Bessemer in 1856.

Smelting is the common chemical process of extracting metal from its ore.

How did we learn to make lamps?

The earliest lamps date back to 70,000 BC, when people in Africa burned tallow (animal fat) in stone cups or shells filled with moss. Later, people discovered coal and crude oil in many parts of the world. So, besides tallow, coal and crude oil were burned in lamps made of stone or clay. The smoke must have been awful!

Candles

As early as 3000 BC, people made the first candles by shaping tallow into a solid stick with a wick through its middle. But by AD 400, the Chinese were making smokeless and odourless candles from beeswax. In 1825, a French chemist named Michel-Eugene Chevreul discovered a way to make odourless candles, called "stearin" candles, from fat. We use stearin candles even today.

Today, candles are available in all colours and shapes.

Gas lamps

One evening, in 1792, a young engineer named William Murdoch was relaxing by the fire at his home in Cornwall. He put some coal dust in the bowl of his pipe, which he placed in the fire. The coal turned to gas, and as it came out of the pipe's mouthpiece, William was amazed to see the gas shine brightly. He realized that "coal gas" could be used to light up lamps! By the early 1800s, most big cities in Europe and the United

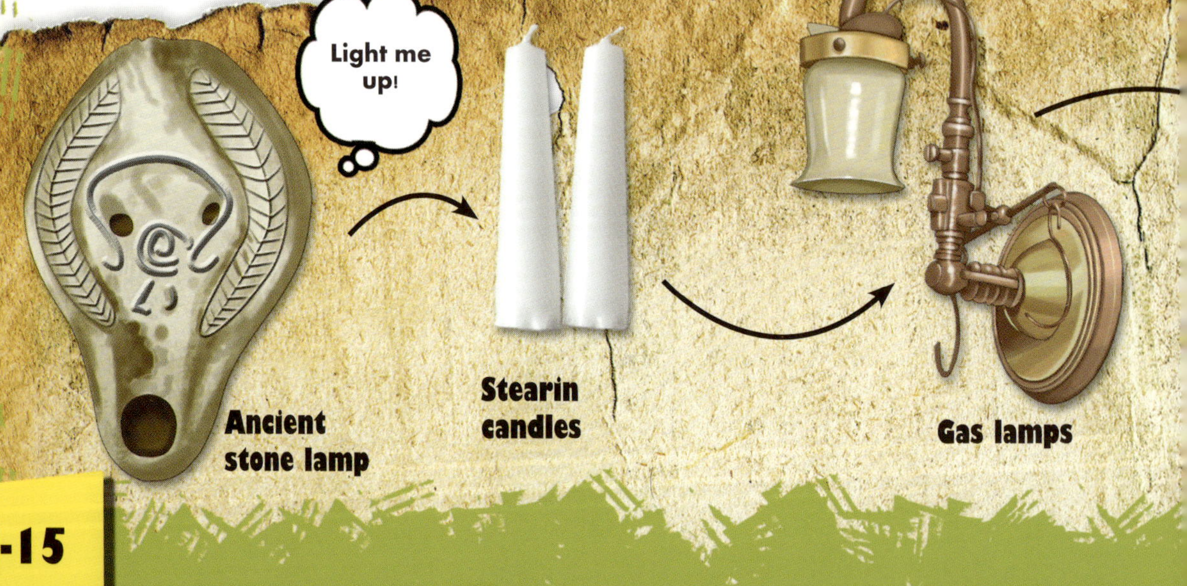

States were using gas lamps to light up streets. In India, Mumbai (Bombay) got its first gas lamps in 1833, thanks to shipbuilder Ardeshir Cursetjee, who installed a plant for producing coal gas at his residence!

Electric bulbs to compact fluorescent lamps

In the early 1800s, Michael Faraday discovered and explained how electricity worked. Following this, Joseph Swan of England and Thomas Edison of the United States, working separately, invented the electric bulb in 1848! After years of court battles over who invented it first, they teamed up in 1883 under the name "Edison and Swan United Electric Company".

Electric light is cleaner, safer, and brighter than light from burning other fuels like gas, oil, and coal. The best are compact fluorescent lamps (CFLs), which use very little electricity.

A traditional kerosene lamp

Old is gold

The streets of London were first lit with gas lamps in 1814. The exterior of Buckingham Palace, London, still uses them for lighting.

Arc lamps

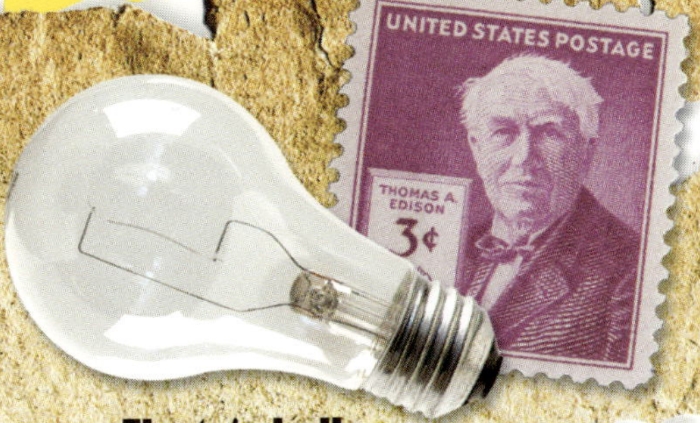

Electric bulb

CFL

How did we find ways to see ourselves?

How do you know what you look like? By seeing yourself in a mirror, of course! Every house has a mirror; you look at mirrors every day, sometimes many times a day. Early humans had no mirrors. The only way they could see themselves was by looking at their images in clear water!

Stone mirrors

The earliest known mirrors were made by polishing clear, smooth, and hard stone. Small, beautiful mirrors made of a stone called obsidian have been found in the ancient town of Catal Huyuk in central Turkey. They were made around 6000 BC! In South America, the Incas of Peru made mirrors from the "Incas-stone". When polished, the Incas-stone looks like shining white steel.

Metal mirrors

Around 3000 BC, people in Egypt were making mirrors by polishing pieces of metals like copper and bronze. Soon, such mirrors were being made in India and China as well. Metal mirrors were costly to make, so not everyone could afford them. These mirrors were small and you could only see your face in them.

Earliest mirrors were made by polishing stone and metal surfaces.

Modern mirrors are made by coating glass sheets with silver or aluminum.

A coating of metal on glass sheets transforms them into mirrors.

A mirror doesn't lie.

Copper was one of the metals used to make mirrors.

Bronze mirrors were used during the Han dynasty, China.

Looking glasses

Around 400 BC, craftsmen in the city of Sidon, Lebanon, learned to make mirrors by sticking leaves of gold, silver or copper to one side of a plate of glass. Such mirrors were called "looking glasses". By the sixteenth century, Venice became famous for its lovely looking glasses. These were made by coating one side of a glass plate with an alloy of mercury and tin. Looking glasses could be made bigger than metal mirrors; but they were still very costly because they used lots of precious metal and took so much time and effort to make.

Modern mirrors

In 1835, German inventor Justus von Liebig found a way to apply a very thin coating of silver to a glass sheet to make a mirror. Liebig's method saved precious metal and made mirrors much cheaper. Today, mirrors are made by coating glass sheets with thin layers of molten aluminium or silver.

Mirrors for stars

Mirrors are used in telescopes to study the stars. The Large Binocular Telescope Observatory, Arizona, has two circular mirrors, each 8.4 metres across. They are the world's largest mirrors.

How did we invent concrete?

From ancient times, people had the idea of using broken pieces of rock (called gravel), along with sand, to make houses and other structures. The problem was how to hold gravel and sand together. They needed to invent a kind of glue – a cement – that could bind gravel and sand. The uniform, hard mass that forms after the sand, gravel, and cement dry is called concrete. So, cement is a key part of concrete!

Presence of lime has been detected in ancient cement.

Binding together for strength!

Early cement and concrete

As early as 6500 BC, people in Syria and the Danube valley in Europe were using a mixture of lime and clay as cement to make concrete walls and floors. In north-western China, people had invented a kind of cement by 3000 BC. Around 2500 BC, Egyptians were using cement to hold together giant stone structures like the Great Pyramid of Giza.

Modern-day cement was invented in 1824.

Wait till I dry up!

THAT'S HOW THINGS BEGAN

Volcanic concrete!

In 300 BC, the Romans added pink-coloured sand to their usual lime-clay cement mixture. The pink sand made the cement very hard when water was poured on it. This sand came from Pozzuoli, near the great volcanic mountain called Mount Vesuvius. So, this cement is called pozzolanic cement. The Romans used pozzolanic cement to build huge stone structures like the Colosseum (AD 82) and the Pantheon (AD 128). Sadly, people forgot the secret of making cement that hardened with water after that…for over a thousand years!

Grand monuments like the Colosseum were held together by cement.

Portland cement and concrete

In 1824, an English bricklayer named Thomas Aspdin was trying to make mortar (the stuff used to join bricks) by heating a mixture of limestone and clay. Accidentally, he overheated the mixture, which became as hard as rock when cooled with water. He had rediscovered the Roman secret of cement that hardened with water! Today, this cement is called Portland cement, and we use it to make concrete.

Flowering idea

In 1867, a French gardener named Joseph Monier was looking for a material to make stronger flower pots. He used concrete with metal embedded in it. Thus, he became the inventor of RCC (reinforced cement concrete), which we use to make giant buildings and other structures!

How did we learn to get power from steam?

From ancient times, we've looked for ways to make our work easier and to travel faster to far-off places. We used animals for carrying heavy things, and to pull carts and carriages. We also invented sailboats. Still, there was a limit to how far and fast we could travel and how much work we could do with animals and sailboats.

And sometimes, the steam will just blow the lid off!

Steam toy

In AD 1, Heron of Alexandria used a round cooking pot to make a strange device called aelopile ("wind ball" in Greek). The aelopile had two tubes at its opposite ends. When water was boiled in the pot, the steam rushed through tubes and made a hollow metal ball turn very fast! But no one saw any use for the aelopile; it remained just a toy.

Hot idea!

Around 1670, a French scientist named Denis Papin noticed that when he boiled water inside a thick-walled, closed cooking pot, the pressure of the steam inside became so great that it forced the lid off. In this way, he invented the first pressure cooker!

The steam engine

Earlier, people in England and elsewhere were mining coal for fuel. Removing water from water-filled mines was a huge problem. In 1698, Thomas Savery made a type of steam pump. It used steam pressure to remove water from the mines. In 1710, Thomas Newcomen modified Savery's pump to make the first steam engine. The two men then teamed up and built many steam engines for mines. The only problem was that their engines wasted a lot of heat.

Not toying around!

The "Toy Train" on the Darjeeling Himalayan Railway is still pulled by an ancient steam engine! The 86 km railway was built between 1879 and 1881.

THAT'S HOW THINGS BEGAN

In 1765, inventor James Watt repaired Newcomen's engine and thereafter made better and more efficient steam engines. These engines could not only pump water but could make wheels turn as well! In the 1800s, steam engines based on Watt's design were used to run all kinds of machines, and to drive ships, carriages, and railway locomotives.

With the steam engine, we were at last able to travel faster to faraway places and to make machines do heavy work for long periods of time.

Heron of Alexandria invented the aelopile in AD 1.

Denis Papin invented the first pressure cooker, which is now on display in Paris.

PRESSURE COOKER

Early pressure cookers used steam to cook food.

I changed the world.

A model of James Watt's steam engine has been built at Loughborough University, United Kingdom.

How did we invent calculators?

In the olden days, when people wanted to add or subtract numbers, they used their fingers or things like pebbles, shells, and seeds.

Abacus

The first counting device was the abacus, which was invented around 2500 BC. At first, the abacus was just a board spread with dust, on which people traced numbers to do calculations. Later, it became a wooden frame with beads threaded on thin wooden sticks or strings. By sliding the beads, people could add and subtract numbers very quickly.

Cowry shell

Early calculators

In 1617, John Napier made a calculator from pieces of bone; it was called "Napier's bones"! Napier also invented a system called "logarithms", which made it much easier to multiply numbers. In 1621, William Oughtred used Napier's logarithms to invent a simple but effective calculator called "slide rule". It worked by sliding one scale over another.

A present-day calculator

Mechanical calculators

Later, people started to make calculators that could do more things with numbers, and do them more quickly. But these calculators were large and complicated, with all kinds of wheels, levers, rods, gears, pins, springs, and other things inside them.

I'm a piece of history.

An ancient abacus

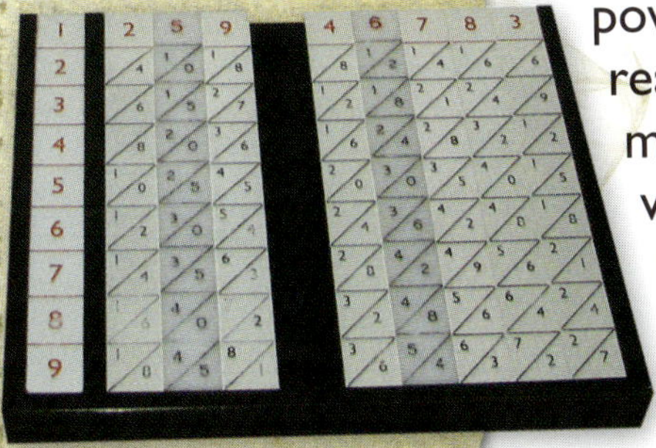

Napier's bones

Early Japanese calculator

Keys to success!

People also tried to create "keys" that would make calculators easier to use, rather than having to push levers and turn wheels! In 1914, Oscar Sundstrand invented a keyboard that made it easy to use calculators. You can see this keyboard on your calculator: ten keys, arranged in three rows (7, 8, 9), (4, 5, 6), and (1, 2, 3), with a zero key below them.

Modern calculators

In the 1900s, people also began to make calculators that ran on electric power. These calculators were really fast and could do all kinds of mathematical operations, but they were still pretty big.

However, everything changed after 1958, when an American named Jack Kilby invented the first electronic "microchip". The microchip was tiny, but it could carry out as many calculations as the big calculators at a much faster speed. Using the microchip, Kilby helped invent the electronic calculator in 1967.

First Keyboard calculator

In 1885, Dorr Eugene Felt of Chicago made the "comptometer" the first calculator with a keyboard, using a wooden macaroni box, staples, rubber bands, wire, string, and meat skewers!

How did we invent the battery?

What's common between a torchlight, car, mobile phone, satellite, hearing aid, laptop computer, and watch? All work on electricity from batteries! A battery is like packaged energy. It gives us energy, whenever needed, in the form of a stream of electric charge (which we call electric current or electricity).

There's a lot of spark in me!

Fur and amber

1

3

Modern-day batteries

What is electric charge?

Around 600 BC, the Greek mathematician Thales found that when a piece of amber, an orangish-yellow fossilized resin, was rubbed against fur, it attracted small, light objects like straw and leaves. The amber even sparked when it was brought near the ground! Thales realized that amber picked up some kind of energy, or "charge", when rubbed with fur. Later, people found other materials that could be "charged" with the same kind of energy. This charge was called electric charge.

Scientists tried to find ways to control and use this electric charge. In 1745, Professor Pieter van Musschenbrock of the University of Leyden, Holland, invented a device called "Leyden jar", which could collect a large amount of electric charge. The trouble was that the Leyden jar released its charge in one great burst, enough to make a big spark and give a severe shock!

The battery is born

In 1791, Italian scientist Luigi Galvani found that he could make a dead frog's leg twitch by touching it with two pieces of metal. He realized that he had somehow created electricity! His friend, Professor Alessandro Volta, worked on this discovery. In 1800, he invented a battery using paper soaked in saltwater and two metal plates. With the battery, people could at last make electric charge flow in a steady stream (electric current) instead of in big sparks!

Later, the work of scientists like Humphry Davy, Michael Faraday, and John Daniel helped make batteries more powerful and dependable. From the large and heavy "lead-acid" battery invented in 1859 to the tiny silver oxide "button cell" invented in 1960, the battery has come a long way!

2

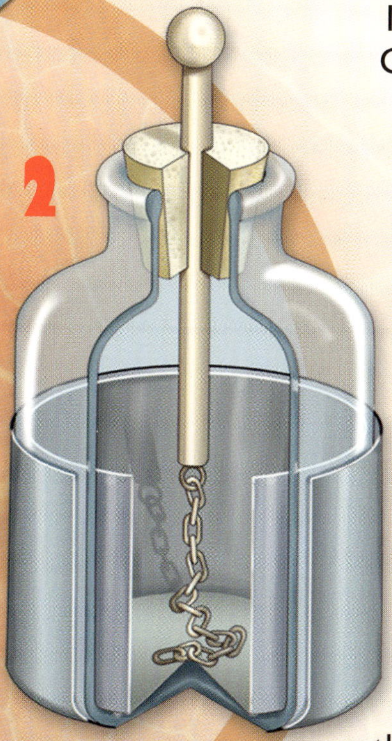

Leyden's jar

World's oldest battery

In 1936, railway workmen dug up a small clay jar near Baghdad, Iraq. It turned out to be a two thousand-year-old battery from an ancient city called Ctesiphon. When scientists poured a little vinegar into the jar, it produced electricity!

How did we invent the refrigerator?

What could be better than a nice, icy drink of lemonade or sherbet on a hot summer day? Nowadays, we can get ice easily, all through the year. Most of us have refrigerators at home, where we make ice and keep things cool. Imagine, then, a time when people could get ice only from frozen lakes and rivers or by collecting snow!

Cooling with ice

Over 2,700 years ago, people in China and Greece collected snow and ice in underground rooms called "ice houses". They stored vegetables, fruit, and wine in these ice houses to keep them fresh through the summer months.

The modern-day refrigerator was invented in 1876 by Carl Paul Gottfried von Linde.

Cooling by evaporation

Long ago, in hot countries like Egypt and India, people found clever ways to cool water and even make ice. They filled shallow pots with water, covered them with moist layers of straw, and placed them in the open at night. By dawn, the water in the pots became so cold that ice formed on the top!

How did this work? When water evaporates (turns from liquid to gas), it takes away heat from its surroundings. You can prove this; wet your finger and then blow on it. You'll feel a cool sensation. So, as the water evaporated from the moist straw, the pots became colder and colder till ice formed.

Cooling by evaporation

In 1834, Jacob Perkins improved on the idea of cooling a vessel by evaporation. Instead of wrapping the vessel with a moist cloth, he surrounded it with pipes filled with ether – a liquid "refrigerant" that evaporates

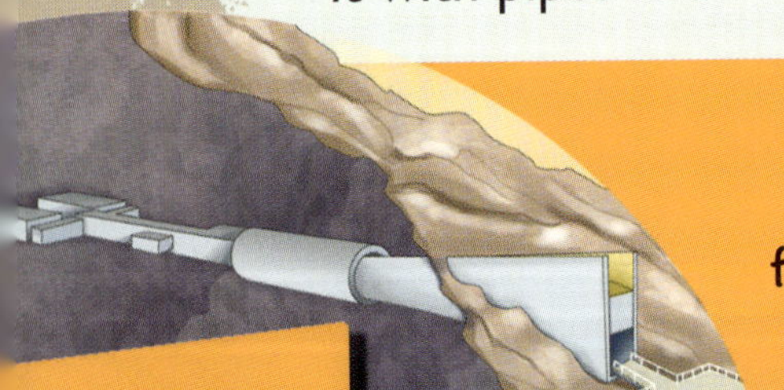

Doomsday Vault

A huge ice house called "doomsday vault" is being dug deep inside a frozen mountain on the island of Svalbard, Norway. It will store and preserve seeds from all over the world just in case some disaster strikes the Earth.

more easily than water. The ether vapour was compressed back into liquid, which was then evaporated again…and again. Thus, Perkins invented the refrigerator.

Safe refrigerants

At first, refrigerators used poisonous refrigerants like ammonia and methyl chloride. In 1929, a non-poisonous refrigerant called Freon was invented. But then, it was found that Freon destroys the ozone layer, which protects the Earth from harmful rays of the Sun. Today, our refrigerators use hydrofluorocarbons (HCFC) and chlorofluorocarbons (CFC).

Excavations have revealed underground chambers used for storage of food.

The Iranians used the yakhchal, an icehouse, about two thousand years ago.

The art of keeping cool!

The Egyptians stored water in pots covered with a moist cloth or straw to cool it.

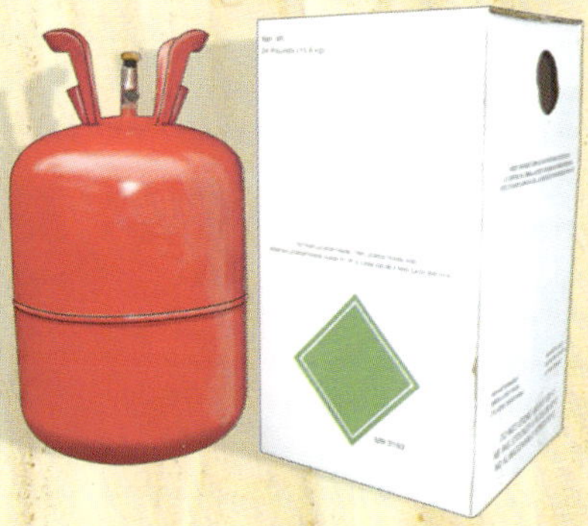

Some refrigerators in the early 1900s worked using a gas called Freon.

How did we invent plumbing?

When people started to live in cities nine thousand years ago, they faced two major problems. One was getting clean water and the other was getting rid of waste. Strangely, we face these two problems even today!

Wasting away.

The earliest drains were made during the Indus Valley Civilization.

The drainage system in Crete was particularly impressive.

Good old smelly days?

In ancient times, water supply meant the nearest well, lake or river. There were no pipes or pumps in those days, so people had to carry water in vessels to their homes. Waste was simply dumped out into the open. As towns and cities became larger, water had to be carried over longer distances for more and more people. The quantity of waste also kept increasing. People realized that waste spread sickness. This led to the invention of pipes and drains.

Well laid out drains have been revealed during the excavation at Lothal, a prominent city of the Indus Valley Civilization.

Was building this draining?
LOWER TOWN

Plumbing

The first pipes for water were invented in the cities of the Indus Valley Civilization around 3000 BC. The pipes were made of fired clay and joined with tar to prevent leaks. The Indus Valley people also built brick drains to carry away waste. The drains were covered with stone or wooden slabs,

The Romans had started building aqueducts in 312 BC.

Metal pipes were found to be long lasting.

Modern-day pipes are made of a durable material called polyvinyl chloride (PVC).

which were removed during cleaning. The drains led to pits where the waste dried out. Soon, other civilizations in the Middle East and Europe began to use pipes and drains. The water and drainage systems in Crete, an island in Greece, were especially impressive. The Romans built great aqueducts (water pipes) to bring water to their cities from far away.

Later, people started to make metal water pipes because these were stronger and lasted much longer than earthen pipes. Lead pipes were popular because lead could be bent easily. The word "plumbing" came to be used for water supply and drainage systems! (Latin *plumbum*, meaning "lead") But later, it was discovered that lead was poisonous. Nowadays, we use steel, cement, special ceramic, and plastic materials to make pipes and drains.

Flushed With History

The Chinese invented the toilet. A two thousand-year-old toilet, complete with stone seat, running water, and comfortable armrests, was found in the tomb of a king of the Western Han dynasty (206 BC–AD 24).

How did we invent paper?

Look at the paper on which these words are printed. Did you know that once, this paper was part of a tree?

Paper's ancestors

Over five thousand years ago, people in China and parts of South East Asia made strips of paper-like material called "tapa" from the pith (inner stems) of plants like mulberry and fig. Around 2500 BC, people in Egypt began to make tapa from the pith of a plant called papyrus, which grew on the banks of the Nile River. Paper gets its name from papyrus. Papyrus was used to write on in Egypt, Greece, and Rome. Strips of papyrus were joined to make papyrus rolls. Some rolls were thirty-five metres long! By the fifth century BC, Greece had large libraries, many of which contained several hundred thousand papyrus rolls.

Egyptian paper was made from the pith of a plant called papyrus.

Today, paper is produced in paper mills.

Wood-pulp paper is born

In AD 105, a Chinese man named Tsai Lin crushed up the bark of a mulberry tree with bamboo fibre, hemp, and flax. He added water, made a pulp of the mixture, and then filtered the pulp and left it to dry. In this way, he invented wood-pulp paper.

Newsprint, a type of paper, is used for frequent publications like newspapers.

Recycle me!

THAT'S HOW THINGS BEGAN

Later, the science of papermaking spread from China to Tibet, India, Central Asia, and Arabia. The Arabs set up paper mills in Cairo, Baghdad, Damascus, Morocco, and Spain. It was hard to get fresh plant fibres in these areas. So the Arabs used rags (cloth waste) instead to make good quality "Arabian paper", which they exported to Italy and other places in Europe.

With the invention of the printing press, the demand for books – and paper – greatly increased. Today, paper mills use complex machines to make all kinds of paper from wood-pulp and rag; but they still follow Tsai Lin's basic method!

Papyrus was also used in Greece for writing on.

Why does paper sometimes turn yellow?

Wood-pulp contains a substance called lignin, which turns yellow in air. To make long-lasting white paper, paper mills remove lignin from wood-pulp. But lignin is left in the pulp when the paper doesn't have to last long – like newsprint! Such paper turns yellow over time.

The crushed bark of a mulberry tree was used for paper-making in ancient China.

Save trees... recycle paper!

It takes about twenty-four trees to make one tonne of printing or writing paper. We should save trees by using less paper and recycling it!

How did we invent money?

Today, we use money to buy and sell everythingfrom pins to pizzas, shoes to ships, chocolates to cars. So how did people manage before money was invented?

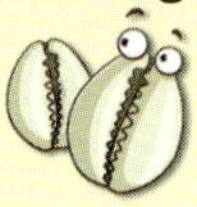

Barter and early money

In the olden days, when people wanted something, they had to give something else in exchange. This system was called the barter system. Soon, people realized barter was easier if they priced things against some special unit – like cowry shells, or snail shells. A goat might cost a hundred cowries; a spear, fifty cowries; and so on. In this way, the idea of money was born. Besides cowries, early forms of money included almonds, beads, beans, feathers, and cows! But it was hard to carry these forms of money around. They also got easily damaged or spoiled.

Coins

After people discovered metals like gold and silver, they thought of using these metals for money and invented coins! The oldest coins were just metal lumps of different sizes and shapes. In Lydia (south-western Turkey), bean-shaped coins called "dumps" were made from a mixture of silver and gold, called electrum. In India, "lump" coins were made from 500 BC onwards.

Anything for a shell?

Feathers and cowry shells were given in exchange for goods in the barter system.

Ancient Greek coins were just lumps of metal.

Imperial Roman coins were made of gold.

Paper money, milled coins

Later, people learned to make circular coins and to stamp patterns onto them. People had a bad habit of scraping the edges off silver and gold coins, melting the metal, and selling it. To discourage this, a way was found to "mill" the coins; that is, to give them a thick, patterned edge! Nowadays, coins are made from steel alloys.

China started printing currency notes in AD 800. Sweden printed the first European paper money in 1601. The great inventor Leonardo da Vinci modified the printing press so that it could produce coins too.

Money matters.

Plastic money

In 1950, American businessman Ralph Schneider launched the first credit card. With a credit card, you can buy things and pay the money later – of course, with an extra charge!

The credit card is often referred to as plastic money.

Coins today are made of steel alloys.

Chinese invented a printing block to make paper money.

Cash

In the fourth century BC, China introduced circular coins with small holes in the middle. These coins were called "cash". The Chinese emperors used cash as their currency, right up to 1916! Even today, we call money "cash".

How did we learn to communicate long distance?

In the old days, people sent messages by beating drums, ringing bells, burning fires, and using smoke signals. But messages could be sent only as far as the fire and smoke signals could be seen, or bells and drums could be heard.

Cellphones rely on electromagnetic waves to deliver messages.

Pigeon mail

Around 2000 BC, Sumerians (people of ancient Mesopotamia) discovered that a pigeon always returned to its nest – no matter how far it might be or how long it had been away! So, they started using pigeons to carry messages from one city to another.

Semaphore

In 1791, Claude Chappe of France invented a clever messaging system called semaphore. Rows of towers were built between distant places. People stood on the towers and used flags or other signals to pass on messages very quickly from one tower to the next.

Graham Bell invented the first telephone.

Drum

Telegraph

In 1830, an American named Joseph Henry found a way by which electric signals could be used, like the semaphore, to send messages down a long wire. Thus, he invented the telegraph. Wires were laid across lands and beneath seas to connect distant places. Samuel Morse invented a system of dots (short electric currents) and dashes (long electric currents) called "Morse code" to send text messages by telegraph. With this, people were able to message one another instantly.

THAT'S HOW THINGS BEGAN

Help! The fire's going out!

People in olden days used smoke signals to send messages.

Telephone

In 1860, a German teacher named Philip Reis made a device that could convert sound into electric current and electric current back to sound. Thus, he invented the first simple telephone! Reis died soon after that, but an American named Alexander Graham Bell was so inspired by Reis's telephone that he built his own telephone in 1876. The telephone became extremely popular. It allowed people to talk to one another instantly, even long distance – provided of course that they were connected by wires.

A telegraph machine

People in Sumeria discovered the use of pigeons as message bearers.

I don't deliver babies...just messages.

The telegraph could send messages using the Morse code.

Wireless communication

In 1887, a German scientist named Heinrich Hertz showed that electric signals could travel not only through a wire but also through the air as "electromagnetic waves". This led to the invention of all kinds of "wireless" communication devices, which we use till today – such as radio, television, and cell phones!

Fax Facts

In 1865, the first "fax" service was started in France. It was used to send pictures to newspapers over telephone.

How did we invent the toothbrush?

One of the first things you do every morning is brush your teeth. So... who invented the toothbrush?

Brushing our teeth is a part of our daily routine.

Early teeth cleaners

People learned the importance of keeping their teeth clean really long ago. In the ancient civilizations of China, India, Babylonia, and Egypt, people plucked little twigs from certain fresh-smelling trees, and chewed the twigs till the ends frayed into rough bristles. They then brushed their teeth with these "chew sticks". Such chew sticks have been found in Egyptian tombs, dating back to 3000 BC.

Beastly toothbrushes!

The Chinese invented the toothbrush. A Chinese book of 1498 describes a toothbrush with bristles fixed to a handle made either of bamboo or bone of cattle. The bristles were actually hairs plucked from Siberian pigs!

In Europe, people cleaned their teeth by wiping them with rags soaked in salt solution. One day, in 1770, William Addis was cleaning his teeth with a rag in a small cell in England's Newgate Prison. He was wondering what he would do after his release when he suddenly had a brainwave. The next day, he saved a small bone from his meal and poked tiny holes into one end of it. He got some animal hair bristles from the guard. He tied the bristles together into little tufts, and then pushed the tufts into the holes in the bone.

This was how Addis made his first toothbrush. After his release from prison, Addis set up a toothbrush factory and did great business. His toothbrush bristles were made of hairs plucked from horses, boars, and cows' tails!

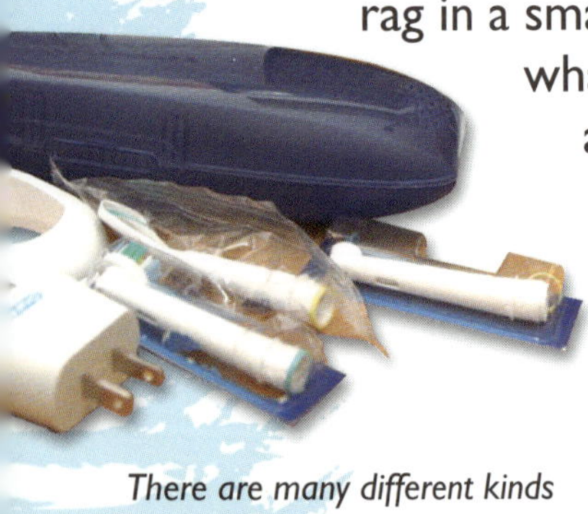

There are many different kinds of toothbrushes available in the market today.

In ancient times, twigs of the neem tree were chewed to clean teeth.

The Chinese invented brushes that were made of bamboo and pig hair!

The modern toothbrush, with nylon bristles, was invented in 1938.

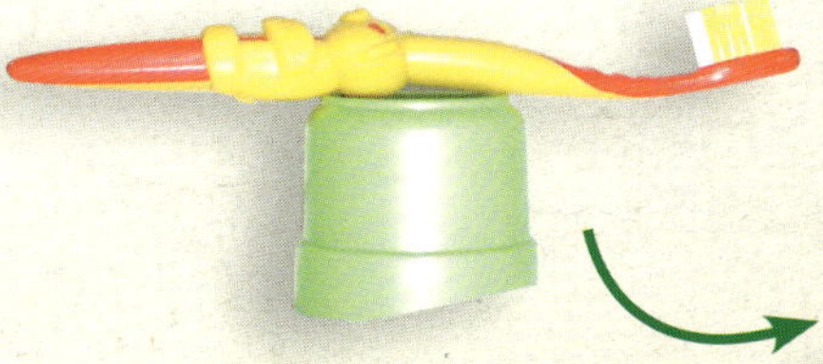

Today, electric brushes are also available.

Your daily breath of freshness!

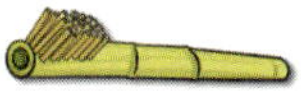

Nylon toothbrushes

In 1938, nylon bristles, or artificial man-made bristles, were invented for toothbrushes. Since then, nylon toothbrushes have spread across the world. Today, there are over two thousand kinds of toothbrushes. Many even run on electric power. One toothbrush model has bristles that change colour when you brush too hard!

Neem Stick

In India, people still use chew sticks made from the neem tree. Neem tastes slightly bitter, but it cleans teeth very well.

How did we learn to sew?

The next time you go to buy a shirt, dress, or pair of shorts, think about this: less than two hundred years ago, there were no ready-made clothes. Across the world, all clothes were sewn by hand!

Hand sewing

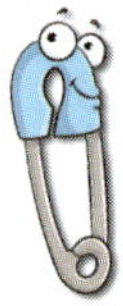

In ancient times, the only way you could wear a garment – say, an animal skin – was by wrapping it around yourself. There were no buttons, clasps or pins to hold it up!

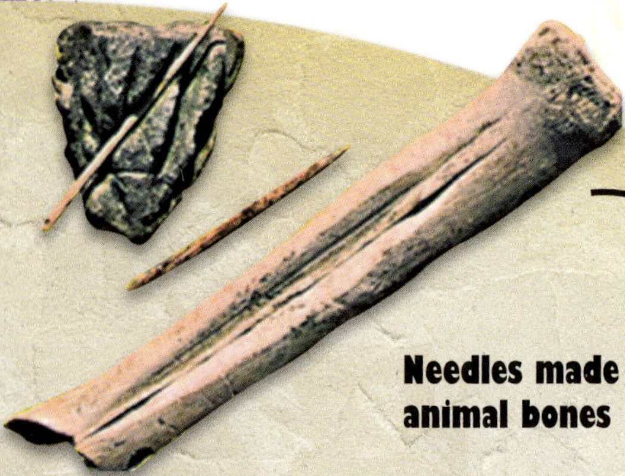

Needles made from animal bones

Giving you that stitch in time!

Howe's sewing machine

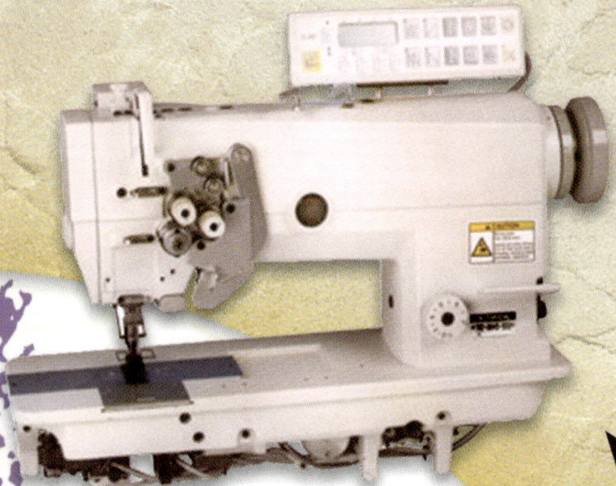

Modern fully automatic sewing machine

Early sewing machine from the company Singer

More than twenty thousand years ago, people invented the needle. The first needles were made of bone. The needle was used to make rows of holes in animal hide (later, in fabric) and to draw and knot thread through the holes. Each knot was called "a stitch". The practice of using a needle to make rows of stitches was called sewing. People could now sew a garment, so that it would not come undone when worn!

Sewing machine

Till the 1800s, all clothes were handmade. People either sewed their own clothes, or got a tailor to sew them for you. As the demand for clothes grew, many people tried to make a machine that could sew clothes. In 1830, a French tailor named Barthelemy Thimonnier invented the first practical sewing machine. But other tailors thought they might lose their jobs because of Thimonnier's invention. They were so angry that they burned down his garment factory and nearly killed him!

In 1834, an American named Walter Hunt made a sewing machine. But Hunt was afraid many tailors would lose their jobs because of his invention, so he gave up the idea! In 1845, another American named, Elias Howe, built on Hunt's idea to invent the first "automatic sewing machine". In 1851, Isaac Merritt Singer made the first sewing machine for home use. Later, he formed the famous "Singer Sewing Machine Company". In 1889, Singer made the first electric sewing machine. Today, clothes are mass-produced across the world by electric sewing machines, which use computer technology.

Flying tailor!

Using its beak as a needle and plant fibres or spider's web as thread, the tailorbird sews the edges of a large leaf together to make its nest!

How did we invent aerated soft drinks?

When you're hot and thirsty, a glass of cold water tastes just wonderful! Often, the water tastes even better when it's got flavour, sugar, and some bubbles, or "fizz", in it. Nowadays, we get such fizzy flavoured water in bottles and small cardboard cartons. They're called "aerated soft drinks".

The journey of aerated drinks began with the humble lemonade.

No-fizz drinks

Across the world, people have always made refreshing drinks at home by adding sugar, salt, spices, and fruit juices to water. In 1676, a French company named Compagnie de Limonadiers began to sell lemonade in Paris. Its workers carried tanks of fresh lemonade on their backs and sold it in cups. However, till the eighteenth century, drinks did not have any fizz in them.

The Coca-Cola bottle was patented in 1977.

Secret of fizz

For thousands of years, people had known that the clear, bubbly water from natural springs was healthy to drink and bathe in. In the eighteenth century, scientists discovered that the bubbles in spring water were mainly carbon dioxide gas. This led to an idea: could carbon dioxide be dissolved in ordinary water to make it bubbly and healthy like natural spring water?

In 1767, Dr Joseph Priestly of England made the first drinkable glass of "aerated water", or "soda" (that is, water with dissolved carbon dioxide). In 1783, a German-Swiss jeweller named Jacob Schweppe started to make and sell fresh soda on a large scale.

By the 1780s, Schweppes had become a rage in London.

Soda fountains

During the early nineteenth century, many American inventors made soda tastier by adding flavours from dandelions, ginger, lemon, kola nuts, coca leaves, and other things. These freshly made flavoured sodas were sold in shops called "soda fountains", which became very popular.

But you couldn't take these flavoured sodas home, because they weren't bottled. Till the end of the nineteenth century, glass bottles were made by hand, and they were expensive. Also, bottle-caps weren't strong enough to keep the fizz inside the soda.

Bottling technologies developed along with methods to make soda.

Cola is the largest selling soft drink in the world today.

Bottled soft drinks

In 1892, William Painter invented a bottle-cap that kept the soda fizzy. In 1899, Michael Owens invented an automatic bottle-making machine. Today, aerated drinks are available everywhere – in bottles and cartons that you can carry home!

William Painter's bottle-cap proved to be a success, as it kept the fizz in soda.

Kettle Cola

In 1886, Dr John Pemberton of Atlanta, United States, created Coca-Cola in a three-legged brass kettle in his backyard.

How did we invent hearing aids?

Many among us, young and old, have difficulty in hearing. Just as we use spectacles or contact lenses to see properly, we use devices called hearing aids to hear well.

How we hear sounds

Sound travels in waves. Our ears are funnel-shaped, so that they can pick up sound waves. The waves enter the ear canal and make vibrations on the eardrum. The eardrum's vibrations are then picked up as patterns by nerves; patterns that our brain recognizes as sounds of different kinds – leaves rustling, birds chirping, music, and so on.

We have difficulty in hearing, if for some reason, our ears cannot gather sound waves properly, or if the nerves cannot pick up the eardrum's vibrations.

Ear trumpet

The earliest hearing aids helped gather more sound waves. The most popular device was the "ear trumpet", invented around two hundred years ago. The ear trumpet had a large horn-shaped mouth that collected sound and funnelled it into the ear through a tube.

Sound throne

King Goa VI of Portugal (1819-1826) had a throne that also worked as a hearing aid. The throne had hollow arms carved to look like lions with open mouths. Visitors had to kneel before the throne and speak directly into one of the lion's mouths. The sound of their voices was carried through the hollow arms to the king's ear through a tube hidden behind the throne!

Modern hearing aids

In the 1870s, Alexander Graham Bell began doing experiments to convert sound into electricity and back again into sound. He wanted to make a device that would help children who couldn't hear. Instead, he ended up inventing the telephone! However, his experiments inspired other inventors to make electrical hearing aids.

An electrical hearing aid picks up sound waves, converts them into electrical signals, strengthens (or "amplifies") these signals, and then converts them back into sound waves, which the wearer can hear. Miller Reese Hutchinson made the first such device in 1901.

Early electrical hearing aids were really large and heavy. A popular 1923 model weighed 7 kg! But they have become smaller and lighter with the improvement of science. Today's digital hearing aids are very powerful and easily fit into the ear.

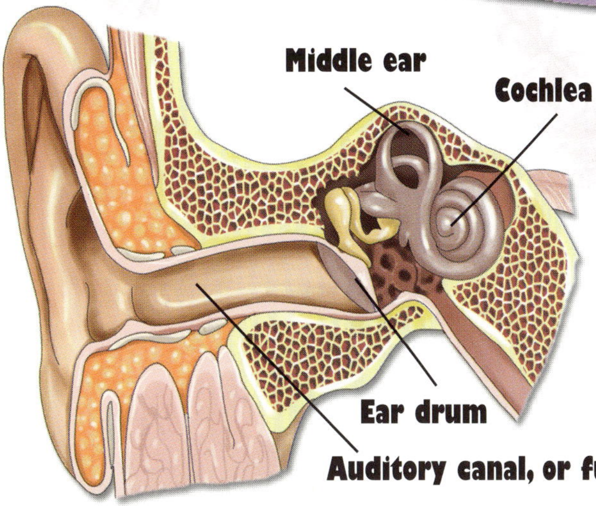

The earliest hearing aids were called ear trumpets.

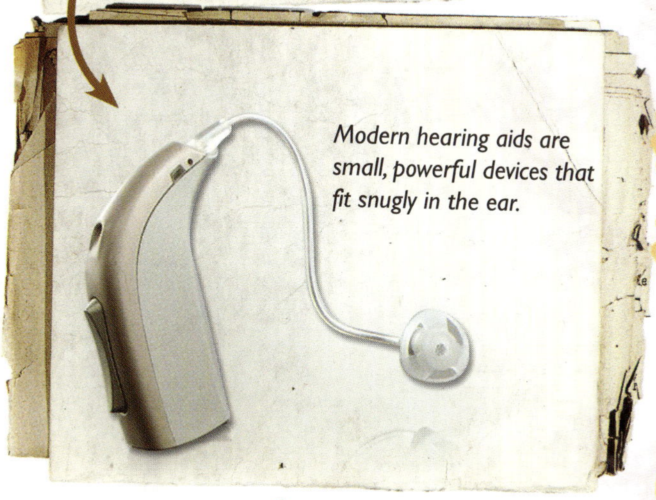

Modern hearing aids are small, powerful devices that fit snugly in the ear.

Make a paper bag

Bag that paper!

We know that paper is made from wood, and that wood comes from trees. So, the more paper we use, the more trees we chop down. We can save trees by using less paper and reusing waste paper. One good way is to make paper bags out of old newspapers! Here's how you can do it.

What you'll need

- A few sheets of newspaper
- Glue, glue stick or sticky tape
- A pair of scissors

How to do it

Step 1
Fold the sheet of paper neatly into three equal parts.

Step 2
Glue or tape the outer two parts together.

Step 3
Fold one end over. Then unfold it again, and fold the corners so that they "line up" with the fold you made earlier.

Step 4
Glue or tape the flap down.

Step 5
Let the glue dry. Your bag is now ready for use!

Index